REVERSING THE DRIFT

Support for Former Trump Supporters

and Quiet Questioners

Ray Hoskins

©2025 Ray Hoskins

Table of Contents

A LETTER TO THE READER..2

INTRODUCTION: WHEN DID YOU START TO BELIEVE?..........6

CHAPTER 1: WHAT MAKES US VULNERABLE?....................12

CHAPTER 2: THE CONDITIONS THAT MADE THE DRIFT POSSIBLE..27

CHAPTER 3: THE DRIFT BEGINS QUIETLY.........................45

CHAPTER 4: CRACKS IN THE STORY.................................57

CHAPTER 5: RETURNING TO YOURSELF...........................70

CHAPTER 6: SPEAKING WITH COMPASSION.....................75

CHAPTER 7: LOYALTY TO WHAT MATTERS NOW...............95

CHAPTER 8: NOW THAT YOU KNOW.............................109

A Letter to the Reader

An invitation to curiosity, honesty, and quiet return

Dear Reader,

I was raised to be, above all, kind. Christians from both Appalachian and German traditions raised me, and I grew up in a rural area. I was fortunate to have had extensive contact through the church and by helping local families with their work, which helped me understand the importance of community.

I left that community, studied history, economics, political science, sociology, and psychology, and followed a lifelong curiosity about humans and how we work individually and in groups. I spent my working career as a counselor, then as a life coach and organizational consultant for human services organizations.

Later, in my private counseling practice, I had clients with narcissistic personality disorder and a few with malignant narcissism. I learned to identify these individuals quickly. I also counseled some young people who had been part of a cult and realized how strong cult-induced beliefs can be. I found it frightening.

So, in the 1980s, when I first became aware of Donald Trump, it didn't take me long to recognize the parallels between my narcissistic clients and him. I read The Art of the Deal and immediately realized the evidence for narcissism in the book.

The years that have followed have confirmed those early impressions. We've watched as promised policies became painful realities: families separated at borders and children placed in detention centers, trade wars that hurt the very workers they claimed to help, democracy undermined by lies about election integrity, and violence encouraged against political opponents.

Most recently, we see our military being used against citizens---those caught up in deportation raids, people here legally who are placed in detention centers, and even deported to their home countries and imprisoned without due process.

Most concerning is how ordinary, decent people---those who once valued kindness, truth, and constitutional principles---have gradually been led to defend things they never would have supported before. Good people making excuses for cruelty. Honest people believing obvious lies. Former Patriots are threatening the democratic institutions they once cherished.

This didn't happen overnight. It happened through a sophisticated process that psychologists call "cognitive capture"---the gradual replacement of someone's independent thinking with ideas that serve someone else's interests. It's what cults do. It's what authoritarian movements do. And it's what happened to millions of Americans over the past decade.

But here's what I want you to know: **if it happened to you, you're not stupid. You're human.**

The human mind can be manipulated by those who understand how it functions. Your psychological defenses can be turned against you. Your values can be hijacked and used as leverage to influence your thinking. Your need for community, significance, and purpose can be exploited by those who offer counterfeit versions of these essential human needs.

If you've begun to notice that something feels wrong---if you're defending beliefs that used to bother you, if the cruelty seems harder to justify, if the slogans sound more hollow---it's not a sign of weakness. **It's your authentic self, trying to come out.**

This book is for those who have drifted from their deeper beliefs, supported an authoritarian, and are ready to find their way back. It aims to help you understand how the drift happened, why it felt so compelling, and how to regain conscious control over your own thinking.

You'll find no lectures here---only understanding. No shame---only compassion for the human journey. No demand that you abandon everything you've believed---only an invitation to examine whether your current beliefs still serve you and the world you want to help create.

If you're holding this book---or scrolling through its pages---you've already done something remarkable: you've stayed curious.

In a world flooded with noise, division, and certainty shouted at high volume, curiosity is a quiet act of courage. It's how we begin to find our way back---not just to truth, but to ourselves.

Thank you for being here. You don't have to do this perfectly. You only have to do it honestly.

Warmly, Ray

Before We Begin: How Did You Get Here?

Tracing your political and emotional path

If you have become, or were, a follower of Donald Trump and the current GOP and are questioning the current direction of our country and our influence on the world, it might be essential to consider how you got here. What were your beliefs and stances before 2014, compared to when you fully supported their agendas and now?

What mattered most?

Do you remember when you believed that character mattered---even in leaders?

And now... something feels off.

Maybe you don't say it out loud. Maybe you still nod along when others talk. You could still post the memes, still wear the hat, and still vote for the ticket. But deep down... something's shifting.

And it's not just about *him* anymore.

It's about *you*.

How did it happen?

How did you go from someone who valued individual liberty to defending a man who demands loyalty and punishes dissent?

How did you go from skepticism of big government to cheering for someone who says, "*Only I can fix it*"?

How did you go from protecting the Constitution to excusing its violations?

This book doesn't ask those questions to shame you. It asks them because you *deserve* to ask them.

You deserve to understand how it happened--- And how to find your way back.

Not to a party. Not to a label. To your*self*.

Introduction: When Did You Start to Believe?

Understanding how belief takes root---and how it can be uprooted

When did you start to believe? Not in a policy or a party---but in *him*?

What was happening in your life at that time? What made his voice feel different than the others?

Did it feel like he understood something you'd been trying to say for years? Or was it more like everyone around you seemed to believe suddenly, and you didn't want to be left behind?

At first, it might have felt like relief. It was as if someone was finally saying what needed to be said. He didn't care what the media thought. He wasn't "polished." He broke the rules. It felt like strength. It felt like rebellion. And maybe, for a while, it felt like the *truth*.

But somewhere along the way, that certainty got harder to hold.

Maybe it was watching January 6th and seeing what "patriotism" looked like when it turned violent. Perhaps it was hearing about family separations and realizing that cruelty had become policy. Maybe it was watching democracy itself being undermined by someone who claimed to save it. Perhaps it was seeing people you respected defend things they never would have tolerated from anyone else.

The slogans stopped landing. The jokes stopped being funny. The cruelty began to feel like a feature, not a bug.

But saying that out loud? Even to yourself? That's not easy.

Because the moment doubt shows up, so does something else: **Cognitive Dissonance**.

Cognitive dissonance is the deep, uncomfortable tension between two beliefs that can't both be true:

"I'm a good person who cares about democracy and human dignity." "I'm supporting someone whose actions undermine both."

"I value truth and integrity." "I'm defending someone who lies constantly."

"I believe in law and order." "I'm excusing attempts to overturn legitimate elections through violence."

That tension isn't just intellectual. It's emotional. It's visceral. And the human brain will do *almost anything* to avoid it.

You may have caught yourself thinking things like:

"They all lie." "He's just fighting dirty because he has to." "The media twisted it." "At least he's fighting for us." "It's not as bad as they're making it sound."

That's not stupidity. That's survival. It's your brain trying to *protect you*---from shame, from loss, from the terrifying thought that maybe... You got it wrong.

But here's the good news:

Feeling that tension doesn't mean you've failed; it simply means you're on the right track. **It means your inner compass is still working.**

If you've ever winced at something he said... If you've ever noticed a policy that didn't sit right with you... If you've ever wondered why the "truth" keeps shifting... If you've ever felt uncomfortable defending things you never would have supported before...

You're not broken. You're just waking up.

And waking up is the first step in the most important journey you'll ever take: **The journey back to yourself.**

What This Book Will Show You

This isn't just a book about politics. It's also a psychology book.

It's about understanding how intelligent, moral people can be gradually led to support things that contradict their most deeply held values.

It's about recognizing the sophisticated methods used to capture human thinking---methods that work on anyone, regardless of education, intelligence, or good intentions.

It's about learning to distinguish between your authentic beliefs and the beliefs that were instilled in you by others for their benefit, not yours.

Most importantly, it's about reclaiming conscious control over your own mind, your own values, and your own choices.

The Promise

If you stick with this process---if you stay curious about your own thinking, honest about your experiences, and open to growth---you will find your way back to yourself.

Not who you were before, but who you're meant to become. Someone who can think independently while engaging compassionately. Someone who can hold complexity without losing their moral center. Someone who can change their mind without losing their identity. Someone who can love across differences without sacrificing their integrity.

That person is still in there. That person has been waiting for you to return. That person is ready to emerge if you're ready to let them.

The journey begins now.

Chapter 1: What Makes Us Vulnerable?

How unmet needs and emotional disconnection created an opening

John didn't think of himself as political.

He was a farmer---fifth generation---on the same patch of Kentucky land his great-grandfather had cleared with mules and muscle. His days were long, his hands were worn, and his pride came not from what he believed but from what he *built*.

He didn't trust politicians. He didn't watch much news. But he knew something was wrong.

His costs were rising. His market was shrinking. His son had moved out of state to find work, and his health insurance bill was higher than his truck payment. He wasn't angry---not yet---but he was tired. And being tired can be dangerous.

Then, one day, someone on the radio said,

"You've been lied to. The system's rigged. The elites don't care about people like you. But I do."

It wasn't John's first time hearing a politician say things like that. But it was the first time it *felt* true.

Sarah's story was different, but the feeling was the same.

She lived in a suburb outside Phoenix, worked in marketing for a tech company, and considered herself well-educated. She had a master's degree, a good salary, and what appeared to be a stable life. But stability felt fragile.

Her industry was changing fast. Younger workers seemed to understand things she didn't. The company culture felt increasingly foreign---new acronyms, new sensitivities, new ways of talking that made her feel like she was constantly walking on eggshells. She wasn't opposed to progress, but she felt left behind by its rapid pace.

At the same time, her teenage daughter was pulling away, rolling her eyes at Sarah's questions and treating her as if she were hopelessly out of touch. Her marriage felt distant. Her church was splitting over social issues. Even her neighborhood was changing---new families moving in who didn't wave back, who seemed to live in their own worlds.

When someone started talking about "taking our country back" and "restoring common sense," it didn't sound like hatred to Sarah. It sounded like *recognition*. Like someone finally saw what she was losing.

Marcus had a different map entirely.

He was a Black man in his forties, a veteran who worked construction in Detroit. He'd grown up believing in hard work, personal responsibility, and the promise that America rewarded both. But that promise felt increasingly hollow.

He had watched his neighborhood struggle for decades while politicians made speeches. He had seen programs that claimed to help but mostly benefited those running them. He had witnessed corruption in city government, inefficiency in social services, and what felt like performative outrage from activists who didn't live in his community.

When he heard messages about self-reliance, not waiting for the government to save you, and the failures of liberal policies---it resonated. Not because he agreed with everything, but because part of it felt *true* to his experience.

He wasn't seeking someone to blame others. He was seeking someone who recognized that the current system wasn't working for him either.

What happens in moments like these?

Why does a single voice stand out amidst the noise---especially one that might have once sounded absurd?

What causes someone to start listening to the loudest speaker in the room?

Sometimes, it's economic anxiety. Sometimes, it's cultural displacement. Sometimes, it's institutional betrayal. Sometimes, it's the simple exhaustion of feeling invisible in your own life.

But there's something deeper, too:

The desire to matter. The desire to feel like your existence has significance. The desire to believe your struggle is *recognized.*

John had worked hard his whole life on that farm. Sarah had followed the rules, earned her degrees, and played by the book. Marcus had served his country and worked to build his community.

None of them asked for praise. But they wanted to know that it all *mattered.*

That their labor, sacrifice, values, and contributions aren't invisible.

Strongmen know how to tap into that. They don't need to offer details. They just need to say, *"I see you. I hear you. You matter."* And when no one else is saying it---when institutions feel distant, and leaders feel performative---that voice can feel like truth.

It can feel like *home.*

That's not stupidity. That's humanity.

And it's one of the most powerful emotional openings in the world.

The Three Things We Need to Feel Whole

Psychologist and educator H. Stephen Glenn once stated that people build resilience and capability when they possess three core self-perceptions:

I am significant. I am capable. I have influence.

People feel confident, curious, and strong when their needs are fulfilled. When those needs go unmet, we drift and start searching for someone or something that can restore them.

For John, his sense of significance was threatened by an economy that no longer valued his way of life. His abilities felt questioned by systems too complex to navigate alone. His influence seemed diminished by forces beyond his control.

For Sarah, her sense of importance was diminished by constant messages that her perspectives were outdated. Her abilities felt challenged by rapid changes she couldn't keep up with. Her influence appeared limited in institutions that seemed to operate by rules she didn't understand.

For Marcus, a sense of importance was denied by a society that only saw him through the lens of grievance or charity. His ability was dismissed by programs that assumed he needed saving instead of opportunity. His influence was limited by a political system that gave him only narrow roles to fill.

Strongman politics offers a shortcut to all three:

It feels like empowerment.

But it's a performance.

It provides just enough dignity to earn your loyalty---and just enough fear to maintain it.

This is why good people say yes to bad leaders. Not because they've abandoned their values--- but because their values were stolen and repackaged as emotional leverage.

You don't drift because you're weak. You drift because you were reaching for something human---and someone appeared pretending to offer it.

How Both Parties Made Us Vulnerable

This didn't happen in a vacuum.

If people felt insignificant, unheard, and powerless, it's because they *were* treated that way. Not just by the political opposition. But by the very parties and systems they once trusted.

For decades, politicians across the spectrum have chipped away at those three critical self-perceptions:

Significance was lost when:

Capability was eroded when:

Influence was undermined when:

The GOP often used slogans that masked elitism. Democrats frequently relied on technocratic solutions that seemed disconnected from everyday experiences. Both, at times, failed to communicate in a way that made people feel **respected**.

Into that emotional vacuum stepped someone who didn't just promise to fix it. He promised to *see* you. To *fight* for you. To *punish* the people who had ignored you.

And when that voice arrived, loud and relentless---it made sense that people listened. Especially when no one else had been listening.

Living Within a Map of Reality

Most of us believe we see the world as it is. But we don't.

We see the world through a map---a set of beliefs, assumptions, experiences, and cultural influences we've gathered over years. This map helps us make sense of things. It filters what we notice. It gives meaning to what happens around us. And most of the time, we don't even realize we're carrying it.

How Our Maps Are Built

Think about it: none of us chose our first map.

Family Foundation: Your earliest map came from your family---not just what they told you directly, but what they demonstrated. How they talked about money, work, and success. How they treated people who were different. What made them proud or ashamed? Whether they saw the world as generally trustworthy or dangerous. Whether they believed individual effort or luck determined outcomes.

John inherited a map that said: *Work hard, keep your word, take care of your own, and the world will respect you for it.* This wasn't just philosophy---it was lived experience across generations.

Sarah's early map stated: *Education and effort lead to security. Follow the rules, be reasonable, and you'll earn your place.* Her parents had risen from the working class to professional status, and their success seemed to confirm the formula worked.

Marcus has a more nuanced map: *America holds ideals worth fighting for, but those ideals aren't always realized. You must prove yourself twice as hard, yet it's still possible to earn respect through service and character.*

Community Reinforcement: Your community---such as the church, school, neighborhood, or social groups---strengthened your map by becoming your "normal." These groups didn't just teach you what to believe; they also showed you *who believes what* and *what kind of people you want to be like.*

If the people you most respected shared certain values, those values became part of your identity. If they distrusted certain institutions, that distrust also seemed natural to you. **Generational transmission**: Maps are passed down through generations, often unconsciously. Sarah's grandfather worked his way up from poverty, and that story of upward mobility became a core part of the family's belief system. Marcus's family took pride in military service and remained cautious about how Black veterans have been treated throughout history.

Trauma and Triumph: Powerful experiences---both painful and positive---become permanent fixtures in our mental maps. The way your family endured hardship, celebrated success, faced betrayals, and the institutions that supported or failed them shape the landscape of these maps.

Cultural Saturation: The movies, books, songs, and stories that surrounded you growing up didn't just entertain---they taught you what heroism looked like, what villains acted like, what America was supposed to be, and what threats were worth fearing.

When Maps Become Rigid

Once we develop our maps, we filter the input we receive from the world through them. Without realizing it, we create a bias that our maps are "right" and prioritize consistency over accuracy in how we process information. This begins at a neurological level. To feel comfortable, we delete input that contradicts our existing perceptions or distort input to make it align with them. Ultimately, we continue to form generalizations or beliefs that may make us even more inaccurate in assessing new information.

In spite of that process, here's what you need to understand: **healthy maps are adaptable.** They evolve as we acquire new information and experiences. However, under stress, fear, or frequent disappointment, maps can turn rigid.

Instead of tools for navigation, they become fortresses for protection.

John's map worked perfectly for decades. But when economic forces beyond his control started destabilizing his way of life, he faced a decision: update the map to reflect global markets, climate change, and technological disruption---or find someone who promised to restore the world his map anticipated.

Sarah's map had served her well throughout college and early career. But when cultural changes accelerated beyond her comfort zone, she could either update her map to include new perspectives---or find voices that confirmed her original map was correct and everyone else had changed.

Marcus's map balanced personal responsibility with awareness of systemic issues. But when political choices seemed to only present extremes---either denying individual agency or dismissing structural problems---he was attracted to messages that simplified the complexity his experience had shown him.

The Emotional Power of Maps

The 20th-century linguist Alfred Korzybski famously said, *"The map is not the territory,"* reminding us that our mental models are simplified versions. They are not the actual world---they are just how we interpret and navigate it.

But what's especially important to understand is that **maps aren't just logical; they're emotional.**

They hold memories, reflect our fears and hopes, and help us understand who we are in the world. Your map doesn't just show what to expect --- it reveals *who you are in relation to what you anticipate.*

When someone questions your map, it doesn't just seem like a disagreement over facts. It can feel like an attack on:

That's why it's so challenging to change maps, even when evidence indicates they need updating.

Maps Under Attack

What made so many people vulnerable to "the drift" was that multiple forces started challenging their perceptions at the same time.

Economic disruption invalidated maps that claimed hard work guaranteed security.

Cultural change challenged maps about family, gender, and community that had seemed stable for generations.

Technological acceleration outpaced the ability of older maps to comprehend new realities.

Institutional failure weakened maps that depended on trust in government, media, or religious leaders.

Demographic changes altered communities, making familiar maps seem less relevant.

When multiple map challenges occur at once, people can feel completely disoriented. In that disorientation, they become vulnerable to anyone who provides a clear, simple map---even if it's based on false information.

The Promise of New Maps

But here's the hope: **maps are updateable.**

Not abandoned---updated. Not by discarding everything you've learned, but by adding new information, new perspectives, and new tools for understanding a complex world.

The strongest people aren't those who never question their maps. They're those who can honestly examine their maps, update them when necessary, and still hold onto the core values that make them who they are.

That's what makes changing beliefs both hard and possible.

Because maps can be inherited, they can also be intentionally chosen. When we become open to questioning whether our map still fits---whether it still reflects what we know to be true---we allow ourselves to access something deeper. Not just new beliefs, but a new connection with truth itself.

I didn't change. The world changed. I didn't move. They moved away from me.

Those are signs of a map becoming fixed---even when the territory no longer matches.

And once the map becomes your identity, *any* challenge to it can feel like a threat.

So ask yourself:

John wasn't a fool. Neither was Sarah nor Marcus. They were thoughtful people facing real challenges. But in their exhaustion, disappointment, or disorientation, they mistook noise for truth---and loyalty for strength. By the time they realized how far they'd drifted, the people around them were often deeper in than they were.

They stayed quiet at first.

Until the silence began to feel like complicity. And then they had to confront the hardest question of all:

"What part of me wanted to believe this... even when the facts no longer added up?"

The truth is, we don't drift because we're stupid. We drift because we're *human*. And humans are wired for three things: **safety, belonging, and meaning.**

When one or more of those are missing, our internal compass begins to spin. We become disoriented. We start seeking the loudest voice, the clearest story, the strongest hand. Even if that hand turns out to be a fist.

Maybe you remember a time when everything around you felt unstable. When everything familiar seemed to be under attack---your job, your values, your community, your understanding of your country. And then someone came along and said, *"It's not your fault. They did this to you. I'll make it right."*

And for a moment, you felt... *seen.*

Isn't that what we all want?

But here's the trap: When someone offers comfort and blame at the same time, they're not helping you heal. They're *trapping* you.

If you've been hooked, you're not broken. You're just human. And it's not too late to return to yourself.

Reflection: Beginning to Explore Your Map

Before moving forward, take a moment to turn inward.

This isn't about trying to fix anything. It's about paying attention. You've just discovered that we all live within a map of reality---one influenced by factors we didn't always choose. Now, you're encouraged to step back and examine your map, not with judgment, but with genuine curiosity.

This is where the work of clarity begins.

🧭 A Simple Exercise

Find a quiet place. Take a few deep breaths. Let your shoulders drop.

Then ask yourself:

Notice what comes up. Don't rush to change anything. Just listen.

Now consider:

You're not trying to dismantle your worldview. You're just learning to see it from an outside perspective.

Maps aren't wrong. They're simply incomplete. Recognizing the boundaries of your map is the first step in deciding how to move forward.

Let that awareness settle. There's no rush. You're already on the path back to yourself.

More Reflection Questions - Chapter 1: What Makes Us Vulnerable to the Drift

When have you sensed something was wrong but chose not to investigate further?

Have the maps you inherited about politics, community, and identity helped you, or are they holding you back?

Chapter 2: The Conditions That Made the Drift Possible

Understanding how we choose what to believe, and why we became vulnerable

Before we discuss the drift---the gradual change in thinking, loyalty, and identity---it's essential to ask a quieter, more human question:

Why were we so vulnerable in the first place?

No one wakes up and says, "Today, I'll follow someone who breaks the rules of truth and decency." These shifts usually don't start with politics. They begin with unmet needs, subtle losses we couldn't recognize, and the slow erosion of the maps that once guided us through the world. They start when something inside begins to feel unstable, and someone offers a story that seems to make sense of it all.

That's the real danger: not just falsehoods, but false certainty amid uncertainty.

The First Cracks

Mark -- The Coffee Shop Mark sat in the corner booth, sipping coffee. "Fox says it's all a setup," a man at the next table said. "Pastor Jim agrees," another man added.

Mark nodded, like always. Fox. Pastor Jim. They were his anchors.

Then a woman wiping the counter said, "Funny how leaders tell you who they are long before we notice."

Mark froze. He didn't know Trump's history. He only knew the voices he trusted.

Dana -- The Facebook Scroll Dana scrolled Facebook every night. Friends posted memes. News links. Quotes from people she liked. QAnon messages popped up too---mysterious, certain, exciting.

She believed most of it.

Then her college roommate typed one simple comment: "Did you check if this is even true?"

Dana didn't answer. Truth was, she hadn't.

Luis -- The Pulpit Luis had always trusted his pastor. If the pastor said God chose Trump, Luis believed it.

Then one night, he read about children taken from their parents at the border.

It didn't feel holy. It felt wrong.

Carrie -- The Talk Radio Voice Carrie listened to the same radio host every day. He was smart. Confident. Angry at the right people.

Then one afternoon he claimed the election was stolen---before any votes were counted.

Carrie gripped the wheel. How could he know that already?

For the first time, she wondered if confidence and truth were the same thing.

Who We Choose to Believe

Many people believed in Trump because of what *trusted voices* said about him. This is called "referential authority." It means we believe something because the source feels right to us. It might be a pastor, a news host, a friend, or even a stranger on the internet who seems to have inside knowledge.

Other people looked at "evidential authority" instead. They wanted facts, history, and proof before making up their minds.

Here's the difference:

Referential authority: *Who* says it matters most. If a trusted person says Trump was chosen by God or is fighting for freedom, that feels like enough. There were and are many religious leaders who served as referential authorities when they endorsed Trump. The Christian Nationalist churches provided major referential authority in support of him.

Evidential authority: *What the evidence shows* matters most. People examine history, records, and facts before deciding what to believe.

The problem? When we only listen to people we trust, we can miss what is true. That's what happened for many people during Trump's rise.

Many Americans entered this past decade already feeling a quiet sense of loss. Some felt pushed aside by an economy that no longer valued their work. Others felt alienated by cultural changes they didn't understand or were told they couldn't question. Some were exhausted---physically, financially, spiritually. Others felt betrayed by institutions they once trusted: churches, schools, the media, and even the government.

What rose in that vacuum wasn't always rage. Sometimes, it was shame. Sometimes, it was fear. It might have been helplessness. Or it was simply the hollow ache of not being seen.

And then someone came along and said, *"I see you. I hear you. You've been betrayed---and I'm the only one telling you the truth."*

That message was powerful, not because it was honest, but because it was emotionally targeted.

When Maps Come Under Siege

Remember: we all carry maps---deeply ingrained beliefs about how the world works, what we can trust, what's dangerous, and who we are within it all. For most of our lives, these maps quietly operate in the background, helping us interpret our daily experiences.

But the past two decades brought something unprecedented: attacks on several parts of our maps at the same time.

Economic Map Disruption

For generations, many Americans followed an economic blueprint that said: *Work hard, develop skills, stay loyal to employers, save money, and you will find security and respect.*

That map helped John's grandfather, who cleared land and built a farm. It also helped Sarah's parents, who moved from working class to professional status. It even helped Marcus's father, who used military service and construction skills to support his family.

But then:

Globalization shifted manufacturing jobs overseas, not because American workers weren't capable, but because labor was more affordable elsewhere.

Technology eliminated entire categories of work---not just manual labor, but middle management, retail, and even professional services.

Financialization caused housing, healthcare, and education to become more expensive while wages remained stagnant.

Corporate culture shifted from long-term employment to short-term contractor arrangements.

The economic map that had guided families for generations suddenly didn't match the territory. People who had followed all the rules found themselves struggling anyway. The map suggested their struggles meant they hadn't tried hard enough. But deep down, they knew that wasn't true.

Cultural Map Upheaval

Cultural maps show us what's "normal," what's evolving, and how quickly change should occur. They help us understand our position in the social hierarchy and what's expected of us.

But cultural change sped up faster than many people's understandings could keep up.

Gender roles that had seemed stable for generations shifted in just one decade.

Family structures diversified in ways that made traditional categories seem insufficient.

Communication norms shifted as social media established new rules for public and private expression.

Workplace dynamics have evolved to include discussions about identity, privilege, and inclusion that many people had never experienced before.

Community traditions that had provided stability---from church attendance to civic organizations---began to decline.

None of these changes were necessarily bad, but they occurred faster than many people could update their maps. When your cultural map feels outdated, you can feel lost even within your own country.

Information Map Collapse

Perhaps most dangerously, the information maps that helped people differentiate between trustworthy and untrustworthy sources started failing.

For decades, most Americans shared a common understanding: newspapers adhered to editorial standards, television news followed professional norms, and experts in universities and government maintained credibility even if you disagreed with them.

But then:

Traditional media lost both economic viability and public trust.

Internet sources proliferated faster than people could develop skills to evaluate them.

Social media algorithms started determining what information people saw based on engagement instead of accuracy.

Partisan media developed to promote worldviews instead of shared facts.

Foreign interference and **domestic disinformation** campaigns deliberately spread false information to create confusion and division.

The result: people have lost their sense of how to tell apart trustworthy and untrustworthy information. When you can't trust your sources, every voice sounds equally valid---or equally suspicious.

How Maps Get Weaponized

We also need to recognize the media's influence---both traditional news and the entire digital ecosystem. Platforms and networks provide people not just with information but with a sense of identity. Fox News didn't just deliver news---it created a narrative. Q-Anon didn't just spread theories---it fostered a feeling of belonging, secret knowledge, and moral purpose. These systems weren't designed to inform. They were designed to keep people engaged, and nothing engages like fear, outrage, and a clear enemy.

"They are lying to you." "Only we are telling the truth." "If you question this, you're one of them."

That isn't reporting; it's psychological manipulation.

And yet---it worked. Not because people were foolish, but because they were *human*.

Into this landscape of disrupted maps, actors who knew exactly what they were doing entered. They weren't just providing political options. They were offering map replacement services.

The Strongman's Map Distribution System

Here's how it worked:

Step 1: Diagnose the disruption *"You feel lost because your old maps don't work anymore. That's not your fault."*

Step 2: Identify the enemy *"People intentionally broke your maps to control you."*

Step 3: Offer a straightforward alternative *"Here's a new map. It explains everything. And it's simple enough that you don't need experts to understand it."*

Step 4: Demand exclusive loyalty *"Anyone who questions this map is working for the enemy. Trust only me."*

This wasn't random. It was a deliberate psychological manipulation aimed at exploiting the specific vulnerabilities caused by rapid change.

Media as Map Distributors

Traditional journalism was meant to help people update their maps with accurate information about changing conditions. But several types of media emerged that did something different: they distributed pre-made maps designed to serve specific interests.

Fox News didn't just report on events---it offered a complete worldview package. Viewers didn't just receive news; they gained an identity, a community, and a simple explanation for complex problems. The map they shared proclaimed: *"Traditional America is under attack by liberal elites, but we're fighting back."*

Talk Radio went even further by building close relationships between hosts and listeners. For people spending hours alone in cars or at work, these voices became trusted friends. The maps they distributed were as emotional as they were informational: *"You're not crazy. Your instincts are right. They are trying to replace you."*

Social media echo chambers use algorithms to reinforce the beliefs people already hold, gradually making them more extreme. If you believed that immigrants were dangerous, you'd see more content confirming that view---until it became a core part of your identity.

Q-Anon and conspiracy networks provided the most alluring maps: secret knowledge that made followers feel special, important, and part of a cosmic battle between good and evil.

These weren't just biased news sources. They were **map replacement systems** designed to make people dependent on a single source of meaning.

The Psychology of Map Replacement

Why did so many intelligent, honest people accept maps that were obviously flawed?

Because map replacement occurs gradually and leverages fundamental human needs:

The Need for Coherence: When your old map stops working, any map feels better than no map. Even a wrong map offers the comfort of certainty.

The Need for Belonging: These new maps fostered communities. People who felt isolated found instant fellowship with others who shared their worldview.

The Need for Purpose: Instead of feeling like victims of economic and cultural change, people could see themselves as warriors fighting for an important cause.

The Need for Simplicity: Complex problems are given simple explanations. Instead of grappling with globalization, technological disruption, and demographic change, people could blame specific villains.

The Need for Specialness: Instead of being ordinary people facing common problems, followers became part of an enlightened minority who could see what others couldn't.

The Role of Legitimate Grievances

Here's what makes this story complicated: **many of the grievances are real.**

Working-class communities had been devastated by economic shifts that politicians from both parties either ignored or actively supported.

Cultural changes had happened so quickly that many people felt disoriented in communities that no longer felt familiar.

Many also believed, or were convinced by others, that as other groups gained strength, their own sense of control and power diminished. It was as if their own power within their trusted community was eroding as others asserted their own individuality or identity.

Institutional failures---ranging from the 2008 financial crisis to foreign policy disasters and government corruption---truly eroded trust.

Media consolidation and polarization have made it truly hard to find trustworthy information.

The issue wasn't that people were angry for no reason. The problem was that their genuine grievances were exploited by actors offering false solutions.

Sarah's frustration with workplace culture changes was understandable---but the solution wasn't to blame immigrants and feminists.

Marcus's disappointment with failed urban policies was valid---but the solution wasn't to buy into conspiracy theories about deep state plots.

John's economic struggles were real---but the cause wasn't a globalist cabal trying to destroy America.

Strongmen are skilled at taking real pain and redirecting it toward fake enemies. They take legitimate concerns and offer illegitimate solutions. They take healthy skepticism and turn it into paranoid certainty.

My Own Susceptibility

I want to be honest: I'm not immune to this either. I've noticed my tendencies and reactions to left-wing media sources that told the story I wanted to hear. Sometimes, I didn't question them closely enough---not because I lacked values---but because I wanted to believe I was on the side that cared, tried, and was still sane.

It's easy to point out bias in others. It's harder to see it in the mirror. However, the truth is that we all live within ecosystems that subtly shape our beliefs, often without us realizing it.

During this same period, I found myself drawn to left-leaning media sources that told stories I wanted to hear. Sometimes I shared articles without thoroughly checking them---not because I lacked critical thinking skills, but because they confirmed maps I already held.

I wanted to believe that I was aligned with the side that valued truth, justice, and democratic principles. When sources confirmed that belief and depicted the other side as entirely wrong, it felt satisfying rather than suspicious.

I realized I was doing what I saw others do: selecting information that supported my current worldview, rather than information that made me think more deeply.

That's the humbling truth: **we all live within information ecosystems that subtly shape our perspectives.** The difference isn't that some of us are immune to manipulation---it's that some of us stay committed to updating our maps when evidence indicates they need revision.

That's why humility matters---not just in who we challenge but also in how we review our maps.

The Infrastructure of Confusion

What made "the drift" possible wasn't just individual vulnerability. It was the systematic construction of an alternative information infrastructure designed to replace critical thinking with emotional loyalty.

This infrastructure included:

Economic incentives that rewarded outrage over accuracy

Technological platforms that amplified division over dialogue

Political strategies that benefited from confusion rather than clarity

Foreign interference aimed at undermining democratic discourse

Domestic bad actors who discovered that chaos was profitable

The result was an environment where **truth became optional, and loyalty became everything.**

People didn't drift toward authoritarianism because they suddenly became bad people. They drifted because the information environment was systematically designed to make drift more likely than clarity.

The Emotional Landscape

Understanding the conditions that made the drift possible also means understanding the emotional landscape people were navigating:

Exhaustion from trying to keep up with rapid change

Anxiety about economic and cultural stability

Loneliness as traditional communities declined

Shame about feeling left behind or confused

Anger at institutions that seemed indifferent to their struggles

Grief for a world that felt like it was disappearing

These emotions made people vulnerable to anyone who offered:

The tragedy is that these needs are truly human. People weren't wrong to seek understanding, community, purpose, and stability. They were manipulated by those who provided false versions of all these things.

The Path Forward

The drift wasn't just about politics; it was about losing trust---trust in each other, our institutions, shared facts, and our ability to disagree without becoming enemies.

People tend to follow the loudest voice that provides coherence when those things fall apart, even if it's untrue.

That's the story many got caught in. That's how good people drifted into defending things they never would have supported ten years earlier.

And now, many of us are starting to feel it.

The unease. The contradictions. The cruelty. The sense that they got pulled into something that no longer reflects who they are.

That moment---that pause, that internal hesitation---is sacred. It marks the beginning of the return. Recognizing the cause of the drift is the first step toward finding a way out.

Understanding how the drift happened doesn't justify the damage it caused. But it does show us that healing requires more than just individual realization.

It requires:

Rebuilding information literacy so people can navigate complex media landscapes.

Restoring economic security so people aren't desperate for quick fixes to complex problems.

Slowing cultural change to a pace that enables map updating instead of map replacement.

Reforming institutions to serve people instead of exploiting them.

Building real community so people don't have to pick between loneliness and extremism.

Most importantly, it calls for **humility** from all of us---recognizing that, under the right circumstances, any of us can be influenced, and that healing requires compassion rather than contempt.

The drift was more than just a political phenomenon. It was a human one.

Understanding it this way is the first step to preventing it from happening again.

Reflection: Who Do You Believe?

Take a few minutes with these questions. There are no right or wrong answers.

1. **Pick one belief you have.** It can be about politics, health, faith, or anything important to you.

2. **Ask yourself where it came from.** Did you believe it because someone you trust said it? Or because you looked for facts yourself?

3. **List your sources.** Write down the people, news shows, or websites that shaped this belief.

4. **Look at the balance.** Are most of your beliefs shaped by *trusted voices* or by *evidence*?

5. **Imagine the opposite.** If this belief turned out to be wrong, what would make you change your mind---a new trusted voice or hard evidence?

This isn't about proving yourself right or wrong. It's about noticing *how you decide what's true.*

Reflection Questions - Chapter 2: The Conditions That Made the Drift Possible

- **Which parts of your inherited maps** were affected by economic, cultural, or technological changes?
- **What real grievances or concerns** made you susceptible to false solutions?
- **How did your information consumption habits** change during times of uncertainty?
- **What emotional needs** (belonging, purpose, certainty, or specialness) were you trying to fulfill?
- **Have you noticed yourself** selecting information that confirms your existing beliefs instead of challenging them?
- **What would healthy map-updating** look like in your life going forward?
- **How can you tell the difference** between reliable sources that help you think and manipulative sources that influence your thoughts for you?

What real community and support **do you need to resist future manipulation?**

Chapter 3: The Drift Begins Quietly

When our maps no longer match reality - and what we do instead of updating them

A moment comes quietly after the cheering fades and the slogans start to sound hollow---a moment when loyalty no longer feels noble; it just feels heavy. The people who once felt certain begin to shift in their seats. They may not say anything, but inside, something has changed.

Carl knew the moment had arrived. Not with a scandal, not with a speech---just a regular evening after dinner. His granddaughter was watching a news clip on her phone. One of the pundits had played back a recent rally. The voice was unmistakable. Loud. Mocking. Cruel. "Look at that face," the leader had said, ridiculing a female opponent. "Would anyone vote for that?"

His granddaughter turned to him, confused and quiet. "Papa," she asked, "why did he say that? That's so mean."

Carl froze. He began to speak, but no words came out. Not because he didn't know what to say, but because he didn't know what he believed for the first time in a long time. A few years ago, he would have agreed with her. He would have told her that character mattered. Leaders should treat people with respect, even if they disagree. But now? He's not so sure anymore. Or maybe he's sure and doesn't want to face it.

He changed the subject, and she went back to scrolling, but he didn't.

When Maps Collide with Reality

Carl was experiencing what psychologists call **cognitive dissonance**---the uncomfortable tension between two beliefs that can't both be true.

I support leaders with good character. I support a leader who mocks people's appearance.

But instead of updating his map to resolve the contradiction, Carl did what most of us do: he tried to make the dissonance go away without changing his beliefs.

This is where the drift starts---not with a dramatic conversion, but with small psychological changes that help us avoid the pain of admitting our maps might need updating.

The Architecture of Avoidance

When reality conflicts with our mental maps, our minds offer us several escape routes.

Denial: *"He didn't really mean it that way."*

Deflection: *"Politicians all do things like this."*

Minimization: *"It's just words. Actions matter more."*

Rationalization: *"He's fighting dirty because the stakes are so high."*

Whataboutism: *"What about the terrible things the other side says?"*

None of these strategies requires us to change our maps. They only need us to change our interpretation of the information that challenges them.

Carl found himself relying on all these excuses. When the leader mocked disabled people, Carl told himself it was taken out of context. When evidence of corruption surfaced, Carl decided all politicians were corrupt anyway. When cruelty became policy, Carl convinced himself it was necessary toughness.

Each rationalization made the subsequent one easier.

The Slow Erosion of Standards

Sarah went through her own kind of drifting.

She had always believed in civility, education, and institutional expertise. Her map said: *"Reasonable people can disagree while treating each other with respect. Experts know more than non-experts about complex subjects. Democratic norms matter more than winning."*

But as her cultural disorientation grew, she found herself drawn to voices that challenged these principles---so long as they appeared to support her concerns.

She began following commentators who mocked their opponents rather than engaging with their arguments. She started sharing articles that confirmed her biases without verifying their accuracy. She found herself cheering when "her side" broke norms that she would have condemned in others.

The drift wasn't dramatic. It was gradual---a slow lowering of standards she barely noticed because it occurred during the service of maps she wasn't prepared to question. Marcus encountered a different variation of the same process.

His inherited maps highlighted personal responsibility, skepticism of government promises, and the importance of strong communities. However, as he became more frustrated with the failure of liberal policies and institutional dysfunction, he started to accept explanations that contradicted his own standards for critical thinking.

He began to believe conspiracy theories that he would have mocked just years earlier. He began trusting sources that told him what he wanted to hear rather than those that challenged him to think critically. He found himself defending positions that conflicted with his own experiences and values---so long as they came from voices that seemed to share his frustrations.

The Psychology of Map Protection

Why do smart, moral people gradually abandon their own standards instead of updating their perspectives?

Because **maps are more than beliefs — they're tied into identities.**

When Carl's granddaughter asked that simple question---"Why did he say that?"---she wasn't just questioning a political stance. She was unintentionally questioning Carl's morality.

That's a huge mental burden for a simple question.

It's much easier to change your standards than to question your whole worldview.

The Escalating Commitment Trap

Psychologists have identified a phenomenon called "escalating commitment", the tendency to continue investing in a failing course of action rather than admit the initial decision was wrong.

This happens because:

Sunk costs feel real: *"I've already defended him so many times. If I change now, what does that say about all those previous defenses?"*

Social pressure grows stronger: *"Everyone in my community supports him. If I express doubts, I'll lose my place here."*

Identity becomes tangled: *"Supporting him has become part of who I am. Questioning him means questioning myself."*

Information sources are limited: *"I can only trust sources that understand why I made this choice in the first place."*

The result is a downward spiral: the more you compromise your standards to maintain your position, the more you must keep compromising to justify the previous compromises.

The Tribal Drift

What makes this process even more powerful is that it rarely occurs in isolation. The drift is often **communal** — entire communities gradually adjusting their maps together.

Carl observed this in his church, his coffee group, and his neighborhood. Conversations that once included diverse viewpoints gradually turned into echo chambers. People who voiced doubts either stopped talking or stopped attending.

The group that stayed behind became more uniform in their views, which made those views seem more normal. When everyone around you is lowering their standards at the same pace, you don't realize the decline.

The Role of Moral Licensing

Psychologists have also identified "moral licensing", the tendency to act less morally after establishing moral credentials.

For many people, their initial support was based on moral reasons: *"I'm supporting him because he'll protect religious freedom / defend working people / drain the swamp / restore law and order."*

That moral framing then turned into a justification for immoral actions: *"Yes, he said something terrible, but he's fighting for a righteous cause."*

The more righteous the cause appeared, the more unjust behavior could be justified in its name.

Three Types of Drift

As I watched people navigate this psychological terrain, I observed three distinct patterns.

The Rationalized Drift

These are people like Carl — essentially decent individuals who have gradually lowered their standards to avoid cognitive dissonance. They didn't become cruel people; they just learned to excuse cruelty in others.

Their internal dialogue sounds like: *"I don't like everything he does, but..."*

The Radicalized Drift

These are people who didn't just lower their standards---they adopted new ones. They started to see cruelty as strength, lies as strategy, and chaos as necessary disruption.

Their internal monologue goes: *"Finally, someone who fights as dirty as they do."*

The Silent Drift

These are individuals who upheld their personal standards but chose not to showcase them publicly. They understood that what they supported was wrong, but they decided to prioritize belonging over truth.

Their internal dialogue sounds like: *"I can't say this out loud, but..."*

All three types represent the same basic phenomenon: **map protection taking priority over map accuracy.**

The Moment of Recognition

But here's what's crucial to understand: **the human conscience is remarkably persistent.**

Even as people drifted, most still had some ability to recognize when something was truly wrong. They just learned to suppress that recognition.

Carl felt it when he couldn't answer his granddaughter's question. Sarah felt it when she realized she was sharing articles she hadn't read. Marcus felt it when he found himself defending positions that contradicted his lived experience.

These moments of recognition---no matter how brief---are sacred. They symbolize the preservation of something genuine beneath all the psychological maneuvering.

The drift starts when we ignore these moments. Recovery begins when we begin paying attention to them.

The Cost of Drift

What Carl didn't realize at first was that safeguarding his political map was harming other aspects of his life.

Relationship with his granddaughter: She stopped asking him questions about current events.

Distrust in his own judgment: He started second-guessing himself in areas unrelated to politics.

Connection to his values: Things that once felt important---kindness, honesty, humility---began to seem naive.

Community relationships: Friendships depended on political agreement.

Peace of mind: The constant rationalizing was exhausting, even when he didn't consciously realize he was doing it.

The drift doesn't just alter your beliefs. It transforms your sense of self.

The Turning Point

For Carl, the turning point happened gradually. Not through disagreements or fights, but through small moments that built up when his conscience wouldn't stay silent.

Watching January 6th and witnessing the violence his "side" had unleashed. Learning about family separations at the border and realizing that cruelty had become policy. Noticing how his own capacity for empathy had diminished. Recognizing that he had become someone his younger self wouldn't recognize.

Integrity isn't just about always being right. It's about how you respond when you find out you're wrong.

That realization doesn't usually happen all at once. It comes in flashes—small clashes between who you thought you were and who you're starting to become. It occurs when you notice you've stopped speaking up about things you used to discuss. When you tell yourself, *"It's just one thing,"* again and again. Until one day, you can't keep track anymore.

The Choice Point

Everyone who drifts eventually hits a decision point—that moment when they must choose whether to keep protecting their maps or start updating them.

Some, like Carl, begin to question. Others, like Harold from his church, double down even more.

Harold seemed to grow more isolated each year, his world shrinking, while his voice became louder and more defensive. It was as if he needed to believe it all—because if he stopped, everything would fall apart.

That decision point is where this chapter concludes and the next starts.

Because recognizing the drift is different from stopping it, and stopping it is different from reversing it.

The question is: **What do you do when you realize your map has been steering you away from who you want to be?**

Reflection Questions - Chapter 3: When Maps Stop Matching Reality

- **Can you recall a moment** when something felt off, but you ignored the feeling?
- **What psychological strategies** (denial, deflection, rationalization) have you used to avoid updating your beliefs?
- **Have you noticed your standards** shifting to fit positions you've already taken?
- **Which relationships or values** have been impacted by your need to defend your political map?
- **What have you sacrificed** to avoid the discomfort of questioning your beliefs?
- **When have you felt** your conscience trying to get your attention?
- **What does it mean** to begin trusting those moments of recognition instead of suppressing them?

- **Are you ready** to stop defending your map and start checking if it still matches the territory?

Chapter 4: Cracks in the Story

When reality breaks through our psychological defenses

It usually doesn't happen all at once.

The shift begins quietly—a fleeting thought, a contradiction you can't quite dismiss. It might be something minor. Maybe it was a joke that sounded crueller than daring. It could have been a comment you'd never accept from anyone else. A policy you would have opposed—if it had come from the other side.

You brush it off. Or you try to.

But it lingers.

And whether you say it or not, you feel it.

Something doesn't sit right.

That's a crack.

Not like you. You're standing on the story you've been part of.

When Maps Meet Undeniable Reality

Carl remembered the first time he truly felt it. It was after the election, after the rallies, after the endless chants. One night, he was watching the news—not on one of the "liberal" channels, but a local station—when they aired a clip from January 6th.

He had seen parts of it before. But this time, he didn't look away. He watched it longer.

He heard the crowd shout, *"Hang Mike Pence. "* He saw the noose, the flags, the anger. He saw police officers beaten with poles, one crushed in a door. And he watched the man they were following---*his* candidate---do nothing to stop it.

He turned off the TV and sat for a long time. Not because he didn't understand what he saw; because he did.

This wasn't what his map had promised.

His map had said: *"We support law and order. We respect the Constitution. We believe in peaceful transitions of power. We honor those who serve. "*

But here were people wrapped in his flag, carrying his symbols, chanting his slogans—doing exactly the opposite of what his map claimed to value.

The cognitive dissonance was too strong to ignore. The contradiction too clear to dismiss. The divide too vast to overlook.

The Moment of Unmasking

Sarah's crack happened differently.

She was at a school board meeting, watching parents yell at a librarian about the books their children might find. The librarian -- a woman Sarah had known for years, who had helped her daughter with research projects and created reading programs for struggling students -- stood quietly as people accused her of corrupting children, having a hidden agenda, and being part of a conspiracy.

Sarah arrived at the meeting prepared to support the parents. Her map showed they were protecting children from inappropriate content. But as she observed the scene, something didn't feel right.

This woman wasn't a monster. She was someone who dedicated her career to helping children learn and grow. The books in question weren't pornography—they were stories about kids from various backgrounds facing everyday challenges.

But the crowd treated her like an enemy. They questioned her motives, her character, and her right to work in their community. They reduced a complex human being to a caricature, then attacked that caricature with self-righteous fury.

Sarah realized something in that moment: **this is what cruelty looks like when it thinks it's justified.**

And she realized she had been a part of it.

Marcus's Awakening

For Marcus, the truth came to light through his nephew—a clever, thoughtful young man studying engineering at a local university.

Marcus had been sharing conspiracy theories about election fraud, deep state plots, and media manipulation. His map told him he was helping his nephew see through lies and think for himself.

But one evening, his nephew sat down to talk with him.

"Uncle Marcus," he said quietly, "I've been looking into some of the things you've been sending me. I wanted to believe them—you know I respect you. But when I trace the sources back, they don't hold up. The evidence doesn't exist. The experts you're quoting aren't real experts. The videos are edited to leave out context."

Marcus began to get defensive, but his nephew kept going:

I'm not saying this to argue with you. I'm saying it because I love you and I'm worried about you. You taught me to think critically, to check sources, and to be skeptical of people who want something from me. But these sources you're trusting—they're asking for your loyalty, your money, and your vote. They're not asking you to think. They're asking you to believe.

Marcus felt a shift inside him. Not because he was ready to abandon all his beliefs, but because he recognized the truth in what his nephew was saying. **The voices he trusted weren't encouraging independence — they were discouraging it.**

His map showed him he was becoming more informed, more awake, more discerning. But he'd been growing more reliant on a limited set of sources that all told him the same story.

The crack wasn't just in the information he'd been consuming. It was in how he understood himself as a critical thinker.

The Anatomy of Cracks

Cracks don't form randomly. They appear when reality can no longer fit into our existing mental maps, despite all our psychological defenses.

Cracks appear through:

Direct Contradiction

When the behavior you're defending clearly goes against the values you claim to hold, making rationalization impossible.

Personal Connection

When abstract issues become personal through people you know and care about---making it harder to dehumanize "the other side. "

Cumulative Weight

When explaining so many things becomes exhausting, and you realize you're exerting more effort in justifying your beliefs than actually examining them.

Trusted Voices

When someone you respect—who isn't trying to attack you—gently points out contradictions you hadn't noticed.

Lived Experience

When your personal observations clash with what you're told to believe about reality.

Moral Exhaustion

When defending your position, you must suppress your conscience so constantly that the suppression becomes intolerable.

Authority Failures

When authorities you looked up to act in ways that fail spectacularly, like an anti-gay preacher caught seducing underage boys.

The Emotional Journey of Cracking

When cracks first appear, they don't seem like enlightenment. They feel like:

Confusion: "I thought I understood what was happening, but now I'm not sure."

Shame: "How could I have been so wrong about something so important?"

Fear: "If I was wrong about this, what else am I wrong about?"

Isolation: "If I change my mind, where will I belong?"

Grief: "I'm losing something that felt important to me."

Anger: *"People I trusted misled me."*

Embarrassment: *"How will I ever face family members who tried to get me to see another point of view?"*

These emotions are uncomfortable—which is why many people try to patch the cracks instead of exploring them. It's easier to find new rationalizations than to face the possibility that your map needs a major revision.

But for those who endure the discomfort, something else appears:

Relief: *"I no longer have to defend things that don't feel right anymore."*

Clarity: *"My conscience was trying to tell me something important."*

Freedom: *"I can think for myself again."*

Integrity: "I can align my beliefs with my values."

Growth: *"I'm learning something important about navigating the world."*

The Different Ways People Respond to Cracks

When reality confronts psychological defenses, people respond in predictable ways:

The Sealers

Some people immediately work to seal the cracks. They find new rationalizations, seek out confirming sources, or dive deeper into their existing information ecosystem. The crack becomes evidence that their enemies are becoming more sophisticated in their attacks.

Harold from Carl's church was a sealer. Every contradiction turned into proof of a deeper conspiracy. Every crack in the story became evidence that the story was more crucial than ever to believe.

The Explorers

Others become curious about the cracks. They start asking questions: *"What if there's more to this story? What if I've been missing something important? What if my sources aren't as reliable as I thought?"*

This is psychologically risky territory because exploring it could lead to the breakdown of beliefs that are core to one's identity.

The Compartmentalizers

Some people recognize the flaws but try to manage them. They might say: *"Yes, he did some bad things, but the overall cause is still right."* Or: *"The specifics might be wrong, but the general direction is correct."*

This method might work for a short time, but it is mentally unstable. Compartmentalized contradictions are likely to grow rather than decrease.

The Shifters

Finally, some people allow the cracks to do their work. They start the slow, often painful process of examining their maps and updating them to better reflect reality.

This doesn't mean discarding everything they believed — it means distinguishing between the parts of their worldview that still serve them and the parts that require revision.

The Role of Community in Managing Cracks

One of the most significant factors affecting how people react to cracks is their community environment.

In rigid communities, cracks are seen as attacks on the group itself. Questioning is considered disloyalty. Doubt is seen as betrayal. The community's typical response to cracks is to seal them rather than to try exploring or understanding them.

Carl experienced this firsthand. When he began to voice quiet doubts, some people in his church looked at him as if he'd switched sides. The message was clear: *"You're either with us completely, or you're against us."*

In healthy communities, cracks are seen as opportunities for growth. Questions are welcomed. Doubt is viewed as part of the journey toward deeper understanding. The community supports members as they navigate the difficult process of belief revision.

Sarah realized this after she began talking to a few friends who shared her doubts. Instead of judgment, she felt relief: *"I'm not crazy. Other people are seeing this too."*

In isolated situations, people often have to face cracks alone, which makes the process more difficult but sometimes more genuine. Without community pressure to fill or examine in specific ways, people can follow their own conscience.

Marcus found this solitude both challenging and freeing. It was scary to doubt beliefs that had given him community and purpose. But it was also liberating to think independently without needing to meet anyone else's expectations.

When Cracks Become Light

The key point about cracks is that **they aren't failures—they are breakthroughs.**

When reality breaks through your psychological defenses, it shows that your capacity to perceive the truth is still active. Your conscience remains present, and your integrity attempts to reassert itself.

The crack isn't the problem. The crack is the answer trying to come out.

Carl didn't cause a scene when his cracks first appeared. He didn't throw away his hat or post angry rants online. Instead, he started listening again—paying attention and noticing what didn't sit right.

He talked to his wife carefully at first. He listened to a friend from work. He asked more questions than he answered.

He didn't say it was "changing his mind." He said it was "getting honest."

And it felt like coming home.

The Sacred Pause

If you've noticed cracks in your story, you're at a crucial moment.

You don't need to take any drastic steps. There's no need to announce or defend your doubts to anyone. Just **stop sealing the cracks and begin exploring them.**

Ask yourself:

You might feel torn between the people you love and the truths you can no longer ignore. Between the community that once gave you a voice—and the quiet voice inside you asking better questions.

That tension doesn't mean you're lost. It means you're still alive inside. It means your inner compass is working to point north again.

And when it occurs, you get to decide which voice to listen to.

Remember: Maps Can Be Updated

Throughout this process, remember what we learned about maps: **they're tools, not absolute truths.**

The goal isn't to create the perfect map—it's to build the ability of conscious map-making. To become someone who can question current perceptions and pursue truth.

Cracks aren't indications that you're broken; they're signs of growth.

They're invitations to become more honest, flexible, aligned with reality, and true to your deepest values.

The question isn't whether you'll experience cracks---it's whether you'll notice them.

The question is: **What will you do when they show up?**

Will you seal them, or will you let them become light?

Reflection Questions - Chapter 4: When Reality Breaks Through

- **Can you recall a moment** when something felt off, but you ignored the feeling?
- **What psychological strategies** (denial, deflection, rationalization) have you used to avoid updating your beliefs?
- **Have you noticed your standards** shifting to fit positions you've already taken?
- **Which relationships or values** have been impacted by your need to defend your political map?
- **What have you sacrificed** to avoid the discomfort of questioning your beliefs?

- **When have you felt** your conscience trying to get your attention?
- **What does it mean** to begin trusting those moments of recognition instead of suppressing them?
- **Are you ready** to stop defending your map and start checking if it still matches the territory?

Chapter 5: Returning to Yourself

Reclaiming your values, voice, and personal power

Reflection: Facing Anger

When you realize someone you trust has misled you, how do you feel? Does it make you angry, embarrassed, or determined? Take a moment to notice how anger appears in you. Anger can signal caring—of wanting something better. The key is not to get stuck there but to let it open the door to change.

There's a kind of peace that doesn't come from winning.

It comes from ending the silent battle within your mind—between what you believe and what you've been pretending to believe. Between the person you've been trying to defend and the person you're quietly becoming.

That peace doesn't come all at once. It arrives gradually, after the shouting stops. After the headlines begin to sound empty. After the friends you once agreed with start to seem distant—not because of what they've done, but because of what you can no longer deny.

It often begins with one quiet question:

What if I've been holding on too tightly to something that no longer supports me?

Carl: The Exhaustion of Pretending

Carl didn't change all at once. It happened gradually, like early spring —quiet, uncertain, and slow.

He first noticed how emotionally drained he was. Not just from the news, but from pretending to be a version of himself that no longer felt genuine. He stopped consuming so much political content. It didn't seem like true information anymore — it just felt like noise.

He started walking more, reading again, and reflecting more— not on politics, but on what mattered to him before everything became a struggle.

That's when he realized how far he had drifted away.

Not toward something evil — but away from something true.

Carl once told his son that true leadership is characterized by calmness and steadiness. That you don't need to yell to lead. That strength is quiet.

He believed it back then. But somewhere along the way, he stopped following it. He began valuing quantity over quality, aggression over humility, and winning over wisdom.

Not because he turned cruel, but because he was tired, scared, and searching for direction.

Sarah: The Risk of Questioning

Sarah's shift began during a sermon. The message was more political than spiritual, seeming designed to divide people rather than bring them together.

She didn't walk out, but something inside her did.

She started questioning things she used to accept without questioning. Her church group became more distant around her. Online friends began to pull away. A few hinted she had "gone soft."

Sarah wasn't gentle; she was just waking up.

She prioritized fairness and valued logic. She believed in listening first before judging. These weren't new values; they were old ones, making a comeback.

And in that return, she began to find herself again.

Marcus: The Courage to Stand Alone

Marcus had always been independent. But somewhere along the way, he had fallen in with the crowd—initially out of anger, then out of habit.

The drift didn't make him hateful. It just made him numb.

His turning point came when he saw someone being mocked at a school board meeting for asking a thoughtful question---no shouting, no hidden agenda, just genuine concern for the kids. And the crowd laughed.

That shook Marcus.

He started to wonder:

When did asking questions start to mean you were the enemy?

He didn't take a side. He wasn't sure if there was one. All he knew was he wanted to think for himself again.

Reflection Questions Chapter 5

- Carl experienced exhaustion from "the silent battle within his mind—between what you believe and what you've been pretending to believe." Can you identify a time when you felt this kind of internal conflict?
- Each person in this chapter drifted "away from something true" rather than toward something evil. What core values or beliefs have you noticed yourself drifting away from?
- Sarah experienced distance from her church group and online friends when she began questioning. Have you ever faced social consequences for thinking differently?
- Carl realized he had started "valuing quantity over quality, aggression over humility, and winning over wisdom." Which of these shifts resonates most with you?
- Marcus wondered, "When did asking questions start to mean you were the enemy?" Do you feel free to ask genuine questions in your communities?

- Sarah found that her "new" values weren't new at all—they were "old ones, making a comeback." What values did you hold before recent years that you'd like to reclaim?

- Marcus chose to think for himself again, even without clear answers. How comfortable are you with uncertainty and independence?

Chapter 6: Speaking with Compassion

How to talk with others still caught in the drift

As you reconnect with yourself, it's natural to want to reach out to those still caught in the same cycle. You notice someone you care about repeating the same angry slogans, defending what's indefensible, or doubling down on a story that no longer makes sense.

Part of you might want to challenge them. Part of you may want to stay silent. Part of you may long to reconnect, but this time with honesty.

You don't want to argue. You want to stay true to yourself.

But how?

Most of us already know what doesn't work. Facts often don't persuade people. Logic alone doesn't cause change. Confronting someone's beliefs directly can lead to shame, anger, or withdrawal.

Why?

Because beliefs—especially those connected to political identity—aren't just opinions. They're rooted in emotion. They're linked to a sense of belonging. They are often reinforced by a strongman who appears to give people exactly what they are missing.

The Real Power of a Strongman

Strongmen rarely succeed by truth. They succeed through emotional manipulation.

They surface when people feel **invisible**, **powerless**, and **ignored.** And they offer something addictive:

You matter. You've been betrayed. I'll bring back what they took from you.

It's not policies that motivate people; it's the promise of **dignity.**

As I mentioned earlier, behind that promise lie three core emotional needs—what psychologist H. Stephen Glenn refers to as the self-perceptions of capability.

- **I am significant.**
- **I am capable.**
- **I can influence what happens.**

These perceptions form the basis of human resilience.

When they are absent, people become vulnerable. When they are provided again—even if falsely—people will hear the voice that influenced them.

Your Job Is Not to Create Doubt

It's easy to think the goal is to make others question their beliefs, but that's not what it's about. The true goal is to **own and share the clarity of your own shift**—without shame, superiority, or pressure.

Changing beliefs doesn't begin with facts. It starts with allowing yourself to doubt without losing your dignity.

Many people have never received that permission.

Carl's Conversation

Carl ran into his old neighbor Jim at the hardware store. They hadn't spoken in a while — not since Carl started pulling away from the groups he used to feel at home in. But Jim brought it up.

You still think the media is full of it, right? They're twisting everything again—just like before.

Carl took a deep breath. He remembered what it was like to be corrected, shamed, or dismissed. It hadn't helped him change; it only made him dig in further.

So, instead of arguing, he responded with a direct **I-message**.

You know, I used to feel that way a lot. It seemed like everyone was trying to twist things. But over time, I realized I mostly listened to voices that made me angry—and not many that helped me think clearly. I got tired of always feeling like the world was falling apart.

Jim looked at him, a bit surprised.

So, do you trust the media now?

Carl shook his head.

No, I don't trust anyone blindly. But I try to pay attention to how I feel after I hear something. If I feel more anger than understanding, I ask myself who benefits from that.

Jim didn't say much after that, but he didn't walk away either.

Carl hadn't won anything, but he hadn't lost touch either. Sometimes, that's the biggest win.

Why I-Messages Work

I-messages speak to your experience without accusing someone else.

Instead of saying:

"You're being manipulated."

You say:

I started to see that I was being manipulated, and I didn't like how it made me feel.

Instead of:

"That's just a lie."

You say:

I thought the same thing—until I saw something I couldn't ignore anymore.

You're not removing power.

You're demonstrating what it looks like to reclaim it.

Reinforcing the Three Self-Perceptions

You're doing something uncommon when you speak to someone respectfully and ask questions instead of attacking.

You are **affirming their importance**—that their experience matters. You are **trusting their ability**—that they can think for themselves. You **recognize their impact**—that they still have a voice, which is significant.

This doesn't guarantee they'll change their mind, but it opens a door.

And sometimes, that's all it takes.

Modeling Another Moment -- Friends in Transition

Karen: "So you don't believe the election was stolen anymore?"

Sarah: "No, I don't. However, I understand why it felt that way. It gave us something to hold onto when everything else felt unstable. But after I examined it on my own, it didn't add up. And I realized I was trusting the people who upset me the most---and that's not how I want to live."

Karen: "So now you believe the media?"

Sarah: "No---I believe in checking things across sources. I believe in being honest with myself when something doesn't line up. That's what changed for me. Not because someone argued with me. Because I finally wondered if there was more to the story."

Sarah didn't attempt to convert. She merely provided a mirror. And sometimes, that's all people need.

Seeing the Other as Being Capable of Growth

Not everyone involved in the movement was initially kind, compassionate, or democratic. Some may cling to longstanding beliefs fueled by resentment or self-interest, while others might have simply gone along to conform.

However, growth is still possible even for those who have never shown their best side. Change doesn't require a perfect past; it just needs enough openness to recognize what no longer works.

If we allow space for transformation, we must **believe that it is possible.**

Not guaranteed, not easy, but possible.

When you speak with dignity—even to someone who hasn't earned it recently—you demonstrate what reclaiming self-respect looks like. You show that strength doesn't come from certainty; it comes from the willingness to grow.

Holding On to Your Shift

If you've begun to wake up, you might feel pulled in two directions. One part of you is gaining clarity, while another part may be afraid to speak, act, or openly embrace that change.

That's common.

Leaving the drift is one journey. Staying out of it is another.

So, how do you maintain your shift?

You don't have to be perfect. You just need to stay honest and aligned with what you now know to be true.

Understanding What You're Really Facing

When someone gets caught in the drift, you're not just managing their political views. You're also engaging with an entire psychological ecosystem that includes:

Their inherited map---beliefs about how the world functions---that are passed down through family and community.

Their defensive mechanisms — psychological strategies they use to avoid the pain of admitting their map might need updating.

Their identity investment - how much of their sense of self is tied to their political views.

Their community bonds---relationships based on shared beliefs

Their information ecosystem includes sources that reinforce their worldview and discourage outside perspectives.

Their unmet core needs---the importance, capability, and influence they want to fulfill through political loyalty.

Understanding this complexity is the first step toward compassionate engagement.

You're not trying to win a debate. You're trying to create a space where someone's true self can safely emerge through all these layers of protection.

The True Power of a Strongman

A reminder: strongmen rarely succeed through honesty. They thrive by employing emotional manipulation.

They emerge when people feel **invisible**, **powerless**, and **ignored**. And they provide something addictive:

You matter. You've been betrayed. I'll restore what they took from you.

It's not policies that influence people; it's the promise of **dignity.**

Behind that promise lie three essential emotional needs:

I am significant. I am capable. I can influence what happens.

As I mentioned earlier, these perceptions form the foundation of human resilience.

When these perceptions are absent, people become vulnerable. When they get something in return—even if it's false—they tend to follow the voice that appears to offer them something.

Your role isn't to undermine that sense of dignity. Your role is to provide a healthier way to restore it.

What Doesn't Work - And Why

Before we discuss what does work, let's clarify approaches that usually backfire.

Fact-Bombing

Presenting someone with overwhelming evidence rarely changes their mind and often causes defensive reactions. When a person's identity is tied to their beliefs, facts can seem like personal attacks.

Moral Lecturing

Telling someone they're supporting something immoral often causes them to defend their stance more passionately because it challenges their self-image as a good person.

Superiority Signaling

Acting as if you're enlightened while they think you're deceived causes shame and resentment. It reinforces their belief that "the other side" looks down on them.

Tribal Switching

Trying to get someone to join your political group instead of encouraging independent thinking just shifts one kind of groupthink for another.

Emotional Manipulation

Using fear, guilt, or anger to influence someone's opinion mirrors the same tactics that caused their original drift.

Public Confrontation

Challenging someone's beliefs publicly makes them defend their position to save face, even if they secretly doubt it.

All these approaches fail because they threaten the person's sense of significance, capability, or influence.

What Does Work - The Foundation Principles

Effective compassionate engagement relies on several key principles:

Lead with Curiosity, Not Certainty

Instead of trying to prove them wrong, focus on understanding how they arrived at their conclusions. What experiences influenced their worldview? What needs are their beliefs meeting? What fears drive their positions?

For example, "What led you to believe that so strongly in the first place?" "You seem convinced that work requirements for Medicaid are essential; help me understand how you became so sure..."

Affirm Their Dignity

Find ways to demonstrate that they are a whole person, not merely a collection of political views. Acknowledge their intelligence, good intentions, and capacity to grow.

For example, "I've known you a long time. You're a very smart guy. I respect you and the ways you look at the world."

Share Your Journey, Avoid Directing Theirs

Share your personal experiences of questioning and change instead of telling others what to think. Personal stories feel less intimidating than abstract arguments.

For example, "I thought that way too for a long time. But then I met a guy at work. He is a legal immigrant from El Salvador. Hardest working guy I ever met. Heck of a nice fellow, too. Great family..."

Ask Questions That Open Rather Than Corner

Use questions that encourage reflection instead of demanding justification. "How did you come to that conclusion?" rather than "How can you possibly believe that?"

I'm genuinely curious about how you reached that conclusion. Were there particular events or strong evidence that influenced your decision?

Create Safety for Doubt

Help them see it's okay to be uncertain, question, and change their minds. Many who are drifting have been told that doubt equals betrayal.

For example: "Heck, I've been rethinking some things lately. For example, I'm not sure it's wise to cut back on Medicaid so much. My mom lives in a nursing home, and I understand she would have to leave if Medicaid gets cut."

Focus on Values, Not Positions

Identify the core values you share and expand on them. Most people want safety, fairness, prosperity, and community—they just have different ideas on how to reach these goals.

For example: "I'm glad we agree that everyone in our community deserves a fair chance. For me, that means not just people who look like me, but others too."

The Art of I-Messages

Again, one of the most effective tools for compassionate engagement is using **I-messages**—speaking from your own experience instead of making claims about theirs.

Instead of: "You're being manipulated." **Try:** "I started noticing I was being manipulated, and I didn't like how that felt."

Instead of: "That's just a lie." **Try:** "I believed that too—until I saw something I couldn't explain away anymore."

Instead of: "How can you support someone so awful?" **Try:** "I used to support him too. But over time, I realized I was making excuses for things I wouldn't accept from anyone else."

Sarah and Her Sister

Sarah's sister Lisa had begun posting more extreme content on social media. Sarah felt a growing distance between them and decided to address it during a family gathering.

Instead of confronting Lisa directly, Sarah decided on a different approach.

Lisa, I've been thinking about something. I realized I was spending too much time on social media, and it was making me feel anxious and angry all the time. I started wondering---am I learning anything useful, or am I just getting worked up? So, I took a break from it for a while.

Lisa looked intrigued. "How did that go? "

It was strange at first. I felt like I was missing something important. But after a few days, I felt more peaceful. Like I could think more clearly. I realized that much of what I was consuming was meant to upset me rather than truly inform me.

"Huh," Lisa said. "I've been feeling pretty stressed lately, too. "

Sarah nodded. "Yeah, I think all this stuff affects us more than we realize. I'm trying to be more intentional about what I put in my brain now. Like, does this help me understand the world better, or does it just confirm what I already think? "

The conversation continued smoothly from there. Sarah didn't criticize Lisa's sources or beliefs. She just shared her own experience and encouraged Lisa to think about her perspective.

The Marcus Method - Questions That Open Space

Marcus tried a different approach with his friend Tony, who had been sending him conspiracy theory videos.

Instead of dismissing the theories, Marcus began asking gentle questions.

Tony, can you help me understand something? You've always been someone who thinks independently. What led you to trust this source?

Well, they're sharing things that the mainstream media refuses to.

That makes sense. I'm curious, though—how do you verify what they're saying? Like, what makes you confident this information is accurate?

They have evidence, documents, and testimonies.

Right, I saw that. I was wondering—have you been able to trace any of it back to the original sources? I tried a few things and had trouble finding the originals.

Marcus wasn't directly attacking the conspiracy theories. Instead, he was encouraging Tony to think critically for himself. He was prompting the types of questions Tony should ask.

Over several conversations like this, Tony became more selective about what he shared. Not because Marcus convinced him, but because Marcus helped him reconnect with his own ability to think independently.

Dealing with Defensive Responses

Even with a caring approach, you might face defensive reactions. Here's how to deal with them:

When They Attack Your Motives

> *You're only saying this because you dislike him.*

Response: "I understand why it might seem that way. I'm not asking you to agree with me. I'm just sharing what I've been going through and wondering if any of it resonates with your experience."

When They Deflect to the Other Side

So, what about all the horrible things Democrats are responsible for?

Response: "You're right that there are problems on all sides. I've been trying to focus on what I can control—my own thinking and choices. What do you think about that approach?"

When They Question Your Loyalty

I thought you were one of us.

Response: "I care about the same things I've always cared about. I'm just questioning whether some of the methods we're using actually serve those values."

When They Shut Down

I would prefer not to discuss this anymore.

Response: "That's totally fair. I appreciate you listening. The conversation is always open if you want to continue it later. "

The Long Game - Building Trust Over Time

Compassionate engagement isn't about quick conversions. It's about building relationships where honest dialogue can occur.

This means:

Practicing patience. Change happens gradually, often during private moments you'll never see.

Be consistent. Your approach should always reflect your values, not just when it's easy.

Being vulnerable involves sharing your uncertainties and growth rather than pretending to have everything figured out.

Be dependable. Respect confidences. Don't exploit their doubts. Steer clear of gossiping about their struggles.

Be present. Stay connected even if you disagree. Don't make your relationship conditional on their beliefs.

Step Back When Needed

Sometimes, compassionate engagement isn't always possible or beneficial. You might need to step back.

Taking a step back isn't quitting. It's understanding you can't make someone question their beliefs, and pushing too hard can damage both of you.

Creating Ripple Effects

When you engage with compassion for people caught in the drift, you're not just trying to change their minds. You're demonstrating what healthy dialogue looks like.

Others are watching, listening, and learning from your example.

Treating political opponents with respect encourages others to follow suit.

When you admit uncertainty and show growth, you demonstrate that strength comes from flexibility rather than rigidity.

Focusing on values rather than positions creates more opportunities for common ground.

Choosing a relationship over being right shows what truly matters.

The Hardest Truth

Here's the harsh truth about compassionate engagement: **you can't convince everyone.**

Some people are unwilling to question their beliefs. Some are too dedicated to their current identity to risk change. Others are trapped in communities where questioning leads to exile.

And that's not your fault.

Your job isn't to save everyone from drifting away. Your role is to be present when someone is ready to climb out. Your role is to demonstrate what genuine integrity looks like. Your role is to create a safe space for doubt and growth. Your role is to love people enough to tell them the truth—gently, patiently, and hopefully.

But the real change? That's what they are responsible for.

And sometimes, the kindest thing you can do is trust them to handle it.

Living Your Compassion

Compassionate engagement is more than just a technique. It's a way of living in the world.

It means:

Choosing love over being right. It's difficult work, but it's essential.

Because each person who reconnects with themselves creates space for others to do the same. Every conversation that opens minds rather than shuts them makes the next one easier. Every relationship that withstands political disagreements shows what democracy really needs.

Every genuine act of compassion lessens the power that demagogues have over people's hearts.

That's more than politics. That's healing.

Reflection Questions - Chapter 6: Speaking with Compassion

- **Who in your life** do you care about that's still caught in the drift?
- **What approaches** have you tried that didn't work, and why do you think they failed?
- **Which of the three self-perceptions** (significance, capability, influence) might the people you care about be protecting through their beliefs?
- **How can you use I-messages** to share your journey without threatening theirs?
- **What values do you share** with people whose political positions you oppose?
- **When you engage with people you disagree with, are you trying to win or trying to understand?**
- **How can you create safety** for others to express doubt or uncertainty?
- **What would it look like** to trust people's capacity for growth rather than trying to force change?
- **How do you maintain relationships** with people whose beliefs concern you?
- **What support do you need** to engage compassionately rather than defensively?

Chapter 7: Loyalty to What Matters Now

Rebuilding community, redefining loyalty, and engaging institutions with wisdom

Releasing the drift can feel unexpectedly liberating.

Even after clarity returns and you start reclaiming your values and voice, there's often a period of quiet disorientation. You might no longer fit into the same conversations. You might no longer laugh at the same jokes, share the same messages, attend certain group meetings, or feel comfortable in the same rooms. The slogans don't have the same impact. The symbols lose their power. And the tribe—whatever form it took—may begin to feel like a place you wandered too far into to come back from fully.

For many, this is where grief appears.

Because part of what's lost isn't just a political identity—it's a sense of belonging, simplicity, and having clear answers to complex questions. A story that once seemed to explain everything, even if it didn't hold up under scrutiny.

What follows is often quieter: the hard work of rebuilding loyalty---not the kind you were asked to give to a strongman or a party, but the kind you give to yourself, your values, and the kind of world you still want to help shape.

When Loyalty Becomes Weaponized

Loyalty has been weaponized. It has been warped into a demand for obedience, a display of allegiance, and a test to see if someone is still "one of us." This is perhaps the most damaging change that happens when strongmen gain influence over communities.

Real loyalty—the kind that builds strong families, communities, and nations—has never been about blind obedience.

Real loyalty is being faithful to what deserves faithfulness.

It's not about always agreeing. It's not about supporting someone no matter what they do. It's about staying connected to what truly matters, even when it's uncomfortable.

Loyalty to truth requires courage. Loyalty to justice demands action. Loyalty to community needs integrity—especially when it's easier to look the other way.

Carl realized this gradually. What he once called loyalty had become nothing more than silence. He told himself he was remaining true to the group, the cause, and the leader. But in reality, he was just avoiding the pain of change.

As he started to see more clearly, he had to face a deeper question: *What do I stand for when no one else is watching?*

For Carl and many others, reclaiming loyalty begins with this shift—**from personality to principle**, from **tribal identity to core values**.

That transition can feel uncertain, but it also creates room for something much more meaningful: loyalty not as a burden but as a choice.

The Map of Healthy Loyalty

What does healthy loyalty look like? It starts with understanding what deserves your loyalty—and what does not.

What Deserves Loyalty

Values that transcend politics: truth, justice, compassion, integrity, courage, wisdom, and service to others.

Relationships built on mutual respect: Family and friends who love you for who you are, not just for your agreements.

Institutions that fulfill their purpose include democratic processes, the rule of law, and systems that protect the vulnerable and serve the common good.

Communities that embrace growth: Groups where you can question, learn, change, and still belong.

Principles that guide good decisions include the Golden Rule, constitutional values, and ethical frameworks that help you navigate complexity.

What Doesn't Merit Loyalty

Personalities over principles: Any leader who demands loyalty to themselves rather than to shared values.

Tribal identity over truth: Groups that require denying reality to remain part of the group.

Winning through integrity: Movements that justify any means to reach their goals

Conformity over conscience: Communities that view questioning as betrayal

Power over service: Institutions that put their self-interest above their mission

Willful harm to others: Denying liberties, services, or other benefits due to perceived injustices caused by others.

Rebuilding Community with Integrity

Many people who leave the drift initially feel lonely. And that's understandable. Much of what was called "community" was really **conformity**—everyone nodding to the same slogans, reposting the same talking points, and reinforcing the same narrative.

But true community can handle questions. It promotes reflection. It creates space for someone to grow and change while still being treated with respect.

What a Healthy Community Looks Like

Carl began to realize this as he became more honest about his changing beliefs. Some people from his old life faded away, but others stayed. And new relationships started to form.

A healthy community includes:

Relationships that withstand disagreements: Friends who can debate ideas without attacking each other's character.

Diversity of thought within shared values: People who want the same core things (justice, security, prosperity) but have different ideas on how to achieve them.

Space for growth and change: Communities where changing your mind is seen as a strength, not a weakness.

Mutual accountability: Groups where members kindly challenge each other to stick to their stated values.

Prioritize contribution over conformity: Communities thrive on collaboration and making a positive impact, not on maintaining ideological purity.

Welcome questions and doubts: spaces where uncertainty is viewed as a natural part of the human journey rather than a threat to group unity.

Finding Your People

Sarah discovered that rebuilding community demands intentionality in where she chooses to invest her time and energy.

She started volunteering with a local literacy program. The work was nonpartisan, but those involved shared her values of education, service, and community growth. She realized that when people come together around common goals, political differences matter less than personal character and dedication.

She also joined a book club that welcomed diverse perspectives. Instead of avoiding difficult topics, they practiced discussing them with curiosity and respect. She learned more in six months of meaningful dialogue than she had in years of consuming confirming media.

Marcus discovered his community through his nephew's engineering program, where he started mentoring young people interested in construction and trades. The focus on hands-on problem-solving and skill building created bonds that went beyond political borders.

You don't need to join a movement to be part of something meaningful.

You should find people who share your core values, even if they have different opinions.

Engaging Institutions with Wisdom

For those who have faced betrayal, disillusionment, or corruption, it can be tempting to lose faith in all institutions. Some institutions do deserve that loss of confidence. However, authoritarianism thrives in that gap—when no one trusts anything, it becomes easier to give loyalty to someone who claims to have all the answers.

The Middle Path: Critical Trust

The goal isn't blind trust or complete cynicism. It's **about critical trust**—being able to evaluate institutions based on their actual performance while remaining open to their potential for good.

Critical trust means:

Evaluating by results instead of rhetoric: Does this institution truly fulfill its declared purpose? Does it protect the vulnerable? Does it effectively solve problems? Does it serve the common good?

Supporting good actors within flawed systems: Recognizing that institutions are made up of individuals, many of whom are working hard to do good despite systemic problems.

Demanding accountability without losing hope: Supporting reform while believing that positive change is possible.

Participating constructively: Engaging in democratic processes, supporting journalism, serving on juries, running for local office—all part of the solution.

Maintaining perspective: Acknowledge that institutions might be flawed, but they are usually better than the alternatives.

Institutions Worth Supporting

Think of the judges who ruled by law instead of popularity during election challenges. The election workers who upheld democratic processes even when threatened. The public libraries that remained places for free thought. The local journalists who continued investigating. The teachers who kept showing up. The healthcare workers who served everyone during a pandemic.

These systems weren't designed to be flashy, but they worked because the people inside them stayed true to their purpose.

We don't need to fall back on blind trust, but we can practice discernment—being willing to look carefully and choose where to place our trust, effort, and voice.

The Practice of Conscious Loyalty

Just as you learned skills for conscious map-making, rebuilding loyalty needs continuous practice and reflection.

Regular Loyalty Inventory

Periodically ask yourself: Does this institution, person, or group still meet my standards and deserve my loyalty?

Values-Based Decision Making

When facing choices about where to invest your loyalty, how does this institution, person, or group align with my values, and are their decisions consistent with my values?

Community Discernment

When deciding if a community is worth your participation, ask yourself: Will joining this community help me stay true to my values?

Loyalty in Action: Three Stories

Carl's Church

Carl's church became more political during the drift years. Sermons shifted from focusing on spiritual growth to addressing cultural issues. People with differing political views were quietly avoided. The community that once felt like a spiritual home started to feel more like a political rally.

Carl faced a decision: completely leave the church or attempt to restore what once made it meaningful.

He chose a middle path. He stayed, but he began asking different questions in Bible study. He shifted conversations to focus on spiritual rather than political topics. He reached out to members who had been marginalized because of their views. He volunteered for service projects instead of political activities.

Over time, he connected with others who shared his desire for a faith community focused on love rather than loyalty to political views. They began meeting informally for prayer and study. Some left the church entirely, but others worked gently to guide the community back to its spiritual mission.

Carl's dedication to his faith drove him to question how his church was expressing that faith.

Sarah's Professional Community

Sarah worked in marketing, and her professional associations had become echo chambers during the drift. Industry conferences featured speakers who reinforced specific political viewpoints. Social media groups shared political content alongside professional advice. Professional networking had become ideological networking.

Sarah began to separate her professional growth from her political views. She stopped discussing political topics at work. Her conversations focused on industry challenges and innovations. She mentored younger professionals regardless of their political beliefs.

She realized that viewing professional relationships as chances to learn instead of as ideological filtering tools helped her build stronger business connections and acquire more useful skills.

Her commitment to professional excellence drove her to resist the politicization of her workplaces.

Marcus's Neighborhood

Marcus lived in a community torn apart by years of political polarization. Neighbors who once helped each other now barely spoke. Community meetings turned into battlegrounds. Local issues became entangled in national political narratives.

Marcus chose to focus on practical problem-solving rather than engaging in ideological disputes. When the local school needed volunteers, he stepped up. When elderly neighbors needed help with yard work, he organized support. When the community center sought fundraising efforts, he dedicated his time and money.

He found that when people worked together on tangible projects, their shared humanity overshadowed political differences. Relationships damaged by political disagreements began to mend through practical cooperation.

His loyalty to his neighborhood compelled him to act as a neighbor rather than a political partisan.

The Ripple Effects of Conscious Loyalty

When you practice conscious loyalty—staying true to values instead of personalities, principles rather than parties—you inspire others to follow suit.

You demonstrate that genuine strength stems from integrity, not from blindly backing flawed leaders.

You show that community can grow through shared humanity rather than shared enemies.

You show what it means to participate actively in democracy rather than just complain about it.

You show that loyalty and growth can go together—that you can remain true to what matters while being open to learning.

Holding On to Your Shift

Intentionally changing ideas is one thing, but sustaining those changes is another.

You will face pressure to fall back on simpler loyalties. The old tribe might try to pull you back, and new tribes could try to recruit you. The complexity of conscious loyalty can feel exhausting compared to the simplicity of blind allegiance.

How do you maintain your commitment to conscious loyalty?

Anchor yourself in values, not positions. Regularly ask: *What kind of person do I want to be? What kind of world do I want to help create?*

Build relationships that encourage growth. Surround yourself with people who inspire independent thinking instead of conformity.

Practice discernment daily. Small choices about where to focus your attention, energy, and loyalty shape who you become over time.

Remember your journey. When you're tempted to revert to unconscious loyalty, recall what it cost you—and what you've gained by choosing conscious faithfulness.

Stay humble about your maps. Continually update your understanding with new information and experiences.

Focus on contribution. The best way to stay grounded in healthy loyalty is to remain focused on how you can serve something larger than yourself.

The New Map of Citizenship

Conscious loyalty ultimately promotes a wider understanding of what it means to be a citizen---not only of a country but also of a community, a democracy, and the human family.

This new map includes:

Engaging actively rather than just consuming passively - aiming to make improvements instead of just complaining about them.

Critical thinking beyond tribal loyalty - Evaluating leaders, policies, and institutions based on their actual performance

Encouraging constructive disagreement rather than destructive division - Learning to debate ideas without attacking individuals.

Prioritizing long-term thinking over short-term wins—considering the impact of your decisions on future generations.

Inclusive communities rather than exclusive tribes - Building bridges instead of walls

Service over dominance - Using your power to uplift others instead of controlling them.

Hope instead of fear—believing that people and systems can improve and actively working to make that improvement happen.

The Ultimate Loyalty

Perhaps the most vital loyalty is loyalty to **the potential for human growth**---your own and others'.

This means:

This is the loyalty that democracy demands. This is the loyalty that healthy communities require. This is the loyalty that can heal a divided world.

And it starts now with your choice to stay faithful to what truly matters—not what's easy, not what's popular, not what's expected—but what's true, what's good, and what helps everyone thrive.

That's more than politics. That's citizenship. That's love.

Chapter 8: Now That You Know

Living your clarity with courage, wisdom, and unwavering commitment to growth

There's no turning back.

You can still walk through familiar places. You can still smile at the same people, sit in the same pew, and nod through the same conversations. But something has fundamentally changed. Not the world—at least not yet.

You.

You no longer see things the same way. You can't unhear what you've heard. You can't unsee the cracks. You can't unknow what it takes to pretend.

You've reached a threshold, even if you can't quite recognize it yet. Now, the question is:

What will you do with your knowledge?

Waking up isn't the finish line. It's a brand new starting line.

It begins a different kind of journey---one without simple slogans, without someone telling you who to be, and without the comfort of borrowed certainty.

It's more complicated at first. More demanding. But also more genuine.

Because once you stop outsourcing your truth, you begin hearing your own voice again. Once you stop acting with certainty, you start living with integrity. Once you stop needing to win every argument, you begin asking better questions.

This isn't about switching teams. It's about outgrowing the need for teams that think for you. It's about becoming someone who doesn't need a tribe to stand tall. Someone who can disagree without turning away. Someone who can care without caving in.

It's about practicing what has always been the hardest to ask of others.

Consistency. Reflection. Courage. Humility. Humanity.

The Weight of Knowing

Now that you understand how maps can be manipulated, you might start seeing manipulation everywhere.

Once you understand psychological defenses, you may notice them in yourself and others.

Now that you understand how good people can drift away from their values, you'll become more aware of your own ability to rationalize.

Now that you've gained the courage to change your beliefs, you'll develop more compassion for those still defending theirs.

This awareness is both a gift and a burden.

Carl felt this deeply. He started noticing things he'd missed before.

How his own thinking could become rigid when he felt threatened. How confirmation bias operated in his mind even after he'd learned about it. How easy it was to slip back into us-versus-them thinking when he was tired or stressed. How much effort it took to maintain relationships across political differences.

Knowledge brings responsibility.

Once you understand how drift occurs, you take responsibility for preventing it again. Once you see how manipulation works, you become accountable for not manipulating others. Once you know better, you're called to do better.

Information Hygiene

Now that you understand how information ecosystems influence your thoughts, you can begin practicing mindful information consumption.

Diversify your sources: Read from different parts of the political spectrum, look for international viewpoints, and focus on primary sources rather than commentary.

Questioning motivations: Asking who benefits when you believe certain information, who profits from your outrage, and who gains power from your fear.

Emotional awareness: Recognizing how different sources influence your feelings and choosing information that promotes thoughtful responses instead of impulsive reactions.

Fact-checking habits: Tracing claims to original sources, seeking corroboration from multiple independent outlets, and distinguishing between news and opinion.

Digital boundaries: Taking regular breaks from social media, unfollowing accounts that consistently make you angry or afraid, and curating your feed to support your growth rather than just confirm your biases.

Reconnect with the people who matter to you: Digital silos keep us apart from neighbors, friends, and family members.

Living Between Certainties

One of the hardest aspects of living consciously is learning to accept uncertainty.

The slide toward authoritarianism offered easy solutions to complicated problems. Awakening involves realizing that the most critical questions do not have straightforward answers.

Sarah learned to live in the space between certainties:

She can support policies she believes in while remaining open to evidence that might change her mind.

She can defend her values while acknowledging that others with different beliefs might have valid concerns.

She could work towards change while recognizing that progress is slow and imperfect.

She can love her country while openly recognizing its flaws.

She can maintain hope despite facing difficult realities.

This isn't relativism—the idea that all views are equally valid. This is humility—the acknowledgment that human understanding is always limited.

The Paradox of Strength

Living consciously requires a different kind of strength than what the drift provides.

Drift strength was performative: loud, confident, demanding agreement from others.

Conscious strength is inner: calm, grounded, and able to stand alone when necessary.

Drift was centered on being right: defending positions, attacking opponents, and claiming moral superiority.

Conscious strength comes from being authentic: acknowledging uncertainty, learning from errors, and growing through difficulties.

Drift strength required enemies: Someone to blame, someone to defeat, someone to unite against.

Conscious strength creates allies: individuals to learn from, work with, and understand.

Marcus realized that conscious strength felt different in his body. Instead of the tense, defensive energy he'd carried during the drift, he felt more grounded, more present, and genuinely powerful.

He didn't have to raise his voice to be heard. He didn't need to attack others to feel powerful. He didn't need to have all the answers to contribute meaningfully to conversations.

Navigating Relationships After Change

One ongoing challenge of living consciously is managing relationships with people at different stages of their own journey.

With Those Still in the Drift

Hopefully, you now see that people caught in the drift aren't evil—they're human beings whose perspectives have been hijacked. This understanding offers both opportunity and responsibility.

The opportunity: To show what conscious living is, create a safe space for personal questioning, and keep love alive despite political disagreements.

The responsibility: To engage compassionately without compromising your integrity, to speak honestly without weaponizing the truth, and to set boundaries when necessary.

Carl realized that his relationships with people still adrift required ongoing adjustment.

Sometimes he engaged in gentle conversations. Sometimes he had to steer talks away from politics. Sometimes he needed to limit contact to keep his peace. Always he aimed to see the person as a whole, not just their political views.

With Those Who Never Drifted

You might need to rebuild relationships with people. you distanced yourself from during your own period of drifting. This requires:

Humility: Acknowledging the potential harm of your past beliefs

Patience: Understanding that rebuilding trust takes time

Consistency: Showing through ongoing actions that your change is authentic

Growth: Demonstrating that you've learned from your experience instead of simply switching sides.

Community Healing

Your local community is the place where you can turn abstract principles into real action.

Participate constructively: Get involved in local government, school boards, and community groups in ways that focus on solving problems rather than political point-scoring.

Supporting strong institutions: Dedicate time, effort, and resources to organizations that effectively serve the common good.

Creating new institutions: Supporting or founding groups, programs, and initiatives that bring people together across differences.

Mentoring others: Sharing your knowledge with those starting their own awakening journey.

The Ripple Effects of Living Consciously

When you commit to living clearly, you join a bigger movement of people choosing awareness over comfort, growth over certainty, and love over fear.

You allow others to question their own beliefs without losing their dignity.

You show that strength stems from flexibility instead of rigidity.

You demonstrate that political differences don't have to ruin human relationships.

You exemplify what healthy citizenship embodies in a democracy.

You demonstrate that hope and realism can exist together.

You represent the potential for human growth and change.

Carl observed these changes in subtle ways. His granddaughter began asking him more in-depth questions about current events. His wife started sharing thoughts she had previously kept to herself. His neighbor began approaching political conversations differently.

He wasn't trying to convert anyone to his positions. He was simply living his values consistently, and that consistency allowed others to reflect more honestly on their own beliefs.

When You

The Ultimate Question

At the end of each day, the real question isn't "Was I right?" or "Did I win?"

The real question is: **"Did I live with integrity today? "**

Did you act according to your true values or from reactive patterns? Did you contribute to healing or division? Did you grow in wisdom or become more certain and rigid? Did you see other people as whole human beings or as political stereotypes? Did you use your power to uplift others or to tear them down?

This is the question that matters. This is the standard that endures. This is the practice that transforms both you and the world around you.

Now That You Know...

You know that maps can be inherited unconsciously or chosen consciously. You know that psychological defenses can protect the ego but also distort the truth. You know that good people can be manipulated into supporting harmful things. You know that authentic strength comes from flexibility, not rigidity. You know that a healthy community requires both individual growth and mutual accountability. You know that democracy requires citizens who can think independently and engage with compassion.

Now that you know these things, you can't unlearn them.

Your knowledge brings responsibility. Responsibility opens up opportunities. Opportunities foster hope.

Not only for yourself, but for everyone whose life you impact.

You are part of the healing this world desperately needs. You are part of the consciousness this moment requires. You are part of the love that overcomes fear, the truth that dispels lies, and the courage that chooses growth over comfort.

This is your moment. This is your purpose. This is your gift to the future.

Live it to the fullest. Live it consciously. Live it in the present.

You Are Not Alone

Finally, remember this: **You are not alone.**

You are not walking it alone.

www.ingramcontent.com/pod-product-compliance
Lightning Source LLC
Chambersburg PA
CBHW020550030426
42337CB00013B/1037